JILL GORDON'S
NEEDLEPOINT

Jill Gordon's NEEDLEPOINT

GLORIOUS TAPESTRY DESIGNS

Foreword by KAFFE FASSETT

FRIEDMAN/FAIRFAX
PUBLISHERS

ACKNOWLEDGMENTS

My first acknowledgments and heartfelt thanks must go to Kaffe Fassett for his unfailing confidence in me, and his support over many years through thick and thin. He has been my constant friend and inspiration.

Through my association with Kaffe I met Maria Brannan—my thanks to her for inspired interpretation and stitching of some of my designs. And my appreciation for her optimism and cheerfulness, sometimes in the face of almost insuperable odds, not to mention constant interruption from my children.

Many thanks also to Hugh Ehrman of Ehrman Kits for his continued support and enthusiasm for my work, and for producing and marketing some of the designs from this book.

I'm very grateful to Juliana Yeo for stepping in and completing some difficult designs at short notice. Also special thanks to Avril Dodd for stitching whenever she had time and for her enthusiasm in helping me to get things done.

Many thanks, too, to Jill Cooper at Paterna Yarns for sending wools off so promptly at short notice and for her cooperation and patience. Indeed I am grateful to Paterna itself for supplying me with all the yarns for the projects in this book.

A special thanks to Judy Spours, freelancing for Merehurst, who has made the whole book possible.

The needlepoint charts in this book are designed to be photocopied and thus increased
to the actual size of the tapestries to be worked. The percentage increase in size needed
when photocopying is given with each chart throughout.

All the designs in this book have been stitched with Paterna yarns.

A FRIEDMAN/FAIRFAX BOOK
Published in 1995 by Michael Friedman Publishing Group, Inc.
by arrangement with Merehurst Ltd
Ferry House, 51-57 Lacy Road, Putney, London SW15 1PR

© 1993 Merehurst Ltd

ISBN 1-56799-215-3

Library of Congress Cataloging-in-Publication Data available upon request.

Designed by Mason Linklater
Charts by Chartwork Design and Print
Edited by Susan Moore
Americanization by Jacquelyn Smyth

Color separations by P & W Graphics Pty Ltd, Singapore
Printed in Singapore by C.S. Graphics

For bulk purchases and special sales, please contact:
Friedman/Fairfax Publishers
Attention: Sales Department
15 West 26th Street, New York, NY 10010
212/685-6610 FAX 212/685-1307

CONTENTS

FOREWORD
by
Kaffe Fassett

When I first met Jill in the early-seventies, to my knowledge she had never painted or done any kind of art work. She was helping out in a large house in the west of England where I was designing and painting with Lillian Delvoryas. I could sense her tangible interest in our work, and she eventually expressed a desire to have a go. Her first paintings, quiet but strong still lifes, made a powerful impression on me. I have never seen someone with little or no art education produce such beautifully composed studies. I snapped up two of her early works and helped her sell many more to enthusiastic buyers. And since we were all working on needlepoint, she had to try her hand at stitching.

———————

A year later, when showing my paintings in New York, I was interviewed by a powerful journalist from the *New York Post*. She spoke to me in her lavishly decorated apartment, and I could hardly concentrate on her questions because of one particular item of her decor—there on a sumptuous brocade couch, among antique embroidered cushions, was a little gem of a needlepoint by Jill Gordon! I felt feverish with pride and appreciation for my new artist friend.

———————

When you think of what we were exposed to as children, it is a miracle that Jill and I were drawn into the world of needlepoint. Drab and boring beige or sage green fields of tent stitch, perhaps with a sad rose in the center, were commonplace. Even huge chairs would be covered in brown, beige and dull green bargello, which appeared to be cut fabric, but in fact entailed countless hours of work. Color seemed to be the least consideration, as was the case with knitting.

In the seventies I began to experiment with color in textiles: at first tasteful antique tones, then playfully complementary ones. I gathered a group of stitchers around me to complete commissions that were coming to my studio. Jill distinguished herself at once with very personal drawing and a delicious sense of color. Together, we worked through wall hangings, wing-backed chairs and headboards in needlepoint. In between the demands of her family and those of my studio projects, she continued to produce a flow of wonderful still lifes and interior views. Two of her early paintings are amongst my most treasured possessions.

When I heard that Jill was producing a book of her own, I wondered how she would fare. I need not have worried for a moment: the result is a blaze of color to light up many a house across the land. Her flowers are anything but sad: their strong, bold forms are wonderfully toned. Her subject matter is unusual, too. She has chosen shoals of fish, and my favorite, water cascading down mossy piles of stones. She had already expressed an intention to render a waterfall in needlepoint, but I couldn't imagine how she would make such an amorphous subject read in stitches. Yet it does succeed with all the charm of early American naïve art.

Jill Gordon is known to many stitchers who shop through Ehrman Kits, and I am sure all her fans will join with me in welcoming her to the world of books with this wonderful explosion of color in stitches.

September 1994

INTRODUCTION

The needlepoints illustrated in this book have evolved over the years, from my first real introduction to the world of art and design. This came relatively late in my life, even though as a child I loved drawing and painting. But at school I was given little encouragement in this field, so that my attempts during that period were limited to the usual pony-mad schoolgirl's drawings of horses, all over my exercise books.

It was not until a chance meeting in 1971 with two American artists, Kaffe Fassett and Lillian Delevoryas, that I received the advice and support needed for me to attempt drawing, painting and design.

After almost a year in Israel, working in a kibbutz, I was wondering what to do next, as the area's level of violence was beginning to alarm me. It was at that point that my brother wrote to say he had met a group of people who might interest me. He was right, and a short time later I found myself employed as a general factotum at Weatherall, in Gloucestershire. My work was as a secretary, gardener, cook, copywriter, childminder, driver and whatever else was required—I still had no idea that I wanted to paint and design.

Both Lillian and Kaffe took part in setting up the workshops at Weatherall. It was mainly through Kaffe's unbounded enthusiasm for involving other people in some form of creative work that the actual workshops had come into being. Wanting to share his creativity, he set about designing large hangings on which everyone there could work.

I helped to stitch these tapestries, after Kaffe had taught us the basic needlepoint techniques. At the same time he encouraged me to start painting, showing me photographs of his own work. So too did Lillian, who, inspired by the wonderful garden at

Weatherall, had herself just taken up painting again after a break of some years.

It was Lillian who bought me my first set of watercolor paints. Neither she nor Kaffe would allow me to become downhearted at my early attempts; instead they kept me at it until I was painting watercolors that I quite enjoyed. I also stitched some small needlepoints I had designed myself, which were framed and sold as pictures or used as inserts in cushions. Twenty years later there was an unexpected sequel to these early endeavors. While looking around Camden Lock, a friend of mine from Weatherall days, Richard Womersley, recognized the little butterfly picture illustrated on this page and bought it back for me.

During the period when I lived at Weatherall I spent as much time as I could on painting, plus a little drawing. Kaffe used to run drawing classes for us, in which his attitude was a revelation to me. Up until that time I had believed as most people do that you were either born with the ability to draw, or you were absolutely unable to because you lacked the gift. With patience however, and the help of others, this changed. I found that given time the majority of us, although not finding drawing easy, can represent any subject accurately enough to enjoy using it for the purpose of design. I owe a

One of my first needlepoint designs, made up as part of a cushion.

large debt of gratitude to Kaffe for this discovery, which has opened many doors for me; and has in fact changed the course of my life completely.

I still find drawing a difficult discipline. Time and again, when teaching needlepoint classes, I see people held back by the same limiting beliefs I once had. Invariably, my pupils say it's all right for me because I can draw—not knowing that I have only learned through repeated attempts. I have also found that observation is the main key to successful drawing and painting; with careful perception of their subject, anyone can learn to draw.

As with other skills, your first attempts probably won't look too good, but if you persist you soon start to achieve results which you can be pleased with.

———————————

It was during this time at Weatherall that I realized painting and design were something I really enjoyed and could actually do, even though this was an area in which I had no qualifications or background. I felt it would be a good idea, though, to go to art college, to learn some basic techniques and to give myself a more solid platform from which to work. I applied as a mature student to Cheltenham College of Art and Design and, somewhat to my surprise, was accepted. Kaffe's own view on this had been that rather than go to college it was better to learn through actual work experience. This may not be true for everyone, but in my case it proved correct, since the College at that time was more interested in abstract art and expressionism than in traditional techniques of working. The outcome was that at the end of the Foundation Year I left and started work with Kaffe in London. He had been commissioned to paint a number of murals, on which I helped him; and though I found the work difficult he was very patient, with the result that I managed to pick up far more basic painting techniques than I had learned at college. In between looking after my family I spent a lot of time painting and stitching for Kaffe at his studio. I also designed work for Hugh Ehrman, now well known for his

mail-order needlepoints. At that time, Hugh was selling work from new designers in many different fields at his first shop in the Fulham Road.

————————

The most valuable lesson I learned from this time of my life was that if you really want to do something, whatever it is, even without formal training you can still do it. All creative work is valuable, no matter how little your first efforts measure up to your expectations. Even now I am my own worst critic, and constantly have to remind myself that if a needlepoint doesn't turn out the way I originally intended, it is still likely to be pleasing in its own right.

————————

The process of conceiving and creating a needlepoint is something I value. I find it fun doing the initial drawings; likewise scaling them up to the appropriate size for the finished work. Looking at these drawings afterwards I often think them satisfying in themselves; and they can always be used as the basis of a painting. After the drawings have been refined and scaled up, the canvas is placed on top and the outlines traced onto it. This is an exciting moment because you can then look at your design references and start choosing colors.

————————

The range of colors in tapestry yarns is absolutely wonderful. One of the hardest things is limiting them to a reasonable number—unless you are doing a work just for yourself, in which case you can choose as many as you wish. It's a good idea to start by deciding on the colors both for your lightest highlights and your darkest shadows, so that you can then work between these extremes. It's a common mistake, and one I still frequently make, to choose colors that don't have enough tonal difference one from another. For example if you wish to use three yellowy greens for a particular leaf, it is no good choosing three greens of different colors but the same shade value— you need to select a dark green, a medium green and a light green, otherwise when they are stitched the effect will be far too bland. This may seem obvious, but it is an easy trap to fall into. If you think of colors as ranging from one to ten, with white as number one and black as ten, you would need to choose three greens approximately of the values two, six and nine for the difference between them to create noticeable light and shadow without contrasting so much that they actually produce a striped effect. All this comes with practice. Before making a final decision there is no substitute for stitching colors next to each other to see how they look.

————————

Painstaking and time-consuming though needlepoint can be, I love the texture of the work and the feel of it as you run your hands across it. By using canvas that doesn't have too fine a gauge, you can see the work progressing swiftly which will give you just the encouragement you need. Needlepoint is quite hard on the eyes, and my first choice would always be to work in good natural light. On dull days and dark evenings I stitch with a spotlight directed on the piece. For choosing colors, though, you do need full daylight. That done, you can work quite happily by a good artificial light; but the colors will still look different. Since those early days at Weatherall in the 1970s I have worked more as a painter and only occasionally as a textile designer, which has undoubtedly influenced my needlepoints. I think what is different about these is that they are designed as part of the actual process of stitching—on the canvas, so to speak. Sometimes a chart or graph has been made later, but only from the finished work. Because my designs develop as they go along, they have a vitality and freshness which would be hard to achieve if they were created on graph paper initially.

———————

Working with freedom and innovation does not mean that I have not been inspired by textiles, wallpapers, china or other decorative art from earlier centuries. The term "tapestry" has many historical associations and shades of meaning. Many

people believe that this term should apply only to woven textiles. In earlier times, however, it described any heavy textile used to cover walls or furniture. It comes from the Old French *tapisser*, to carpet, and in my view can be freely applied to any textile covering, whether woven or stitched.

———————

I also think the older use of the word could quite as well describe the pieces in this book. William Morris, the British arts and crafts theorist of the nineteenth century, summed up more than adequately what I have tried to do here when he likened tapestry to a mosaic made up of colored threads. The French architect Le Corbusier also put it aptly in referring to tapestries as nomadic murals, decorative but movable and interchangeable.

———————

This flexibility of use is something I have tried to reflect in my designs, along with the adaptable nature of my many references and sources of inspiration. I hope this book inspires you to look afresh at the subjects that appeal to you, and gives you the motivation and confidence to stitch these designs and to create ones of your own.

———————

Note: Measurements in this book are given in inches; to calculate width and length in centimeters, multiply the number of inches by 2.54.

F L O W E R S

When I started to paint, at approximately the age of twenty-one, flowers were my foremost inspiration. My very first painting proper was of a vase of polyanthus surrounded by an Indian patterned fabric in acid yellow. To my surprise it was much admired; I had thought it pretty awful considering the grand aspirations with which I'd set to work. This taught me the valuable lesson that whatever the end result, it can still have worth and give much pleasure to others.

I admit that I have never been satisfied with my own finished works, whether drawings, needlepoints or paintings. But I've come to see this as a bonus rather than a deterrent, since it inspires me each time to see if I can come closer to my goal. Ever since my first attempts, and the discovery that people actually wanted to buy them, I've been glad of any chance to attempt the same subject again, usually coming closer to my original intentions and always learning more about painting.

————————

When planning your own needlepoint designs one method is to make sketches and watercolors of the actual flower or plant you want to work from. I do not think there is any flower, or anything else in nature, that I do not see as beautiful in some way. It is difficult to say which are my favorites, though nasturtiums leap to mind for the creeper-like form of the whole plant, with their wonderful leaves and flowers, closely followed by roses, orchids, chrysanthemums and hellebores.

————————

Other than nature itself, a useful design reference is the body of extremely beautiful and precise botanical paintings from the seventeenth, eighteenth and early nineteenth centuries. To look at the work of artists such as Redoute, Robert Thornton, Georg Ehret and the Bauer brothers, is to discover that much of the transcription from flower to wool has been done for you. The clarity of detail and color is such that you can stitch the subjects almost as they are painted.

————————

A common mistake, which puts off many people when they first think of stitching their own designs, is to feel they must put in every little detail. It is much more effective to half close your eyes so that you can see the distinguishing features of what you want to depict - the differences in light and shadow that it is essential to capture. Observation - this cannot be stressed too often in my opinion - is the greatest part of any successful creative work. We all think we know what a particular object looks like. But when you look at it carefully it is interesting to see what wrong ideas you may have.

————————

I usually approach a subject by doing some rough sketches, putting in a watercolor wash to remind myself of the colors I am seeing. While working I always have reference material around me, whether a drawing or photograph such as the front of a seed packet or a landscape reference, depending on the subject. I also refer constantly to these sources when stitching, seeking to capture highlights, areas of shadow, and anything else that really defines the subject.

————————

Then I decide on the scale of the piece: would it be best as a hanging or a large picture, or would I like it to be used as a cushion or pillow? This done, I measure out the design on a piece of graph paper and do a line drawing to scale in pencil from my preliminary sketches. Once all the shapes and sizes look right I go over the pencil lines in black ink, heavily enough to be able to trace them onto the piece of canvas when this has been placed on top of the line drawing.

———————————

Next, the canvas should be cut to the size required, that is allowing at least two inches of surplus around the measurements of the finished stitched area. This is so that afterwards the piece can be properly stretched (see Appendix, pp. 156-7). When tracing the drawing through onto the canvas it is important to use a good-quality permanent marker. This is important so that when you dampen the canvas while stretching it, the ink will not run through into the yarn.

———————————

Fairly large-gauge canvas—no more than 10 holes per inch—has been used for all the designs in this book. An even larger weave—7.6 holes per inch—has been used for the Irises and Delphiniums hanging (p. 37), the Heraldic cushion (p. 87) and the Hollyhock screen (p. 19). Though not large, the Heraldic cushion requires little detail, and the screen and hanging are big enough to allow a complex design even on this gauge of canvas.

———————————

Broadly speaking though, the more definition you want, the greater the number of holes you will need per inch. An ob-vious drawback is that the stitching will take that much longer. I think it very important that you have the satisfaction of being able to complete the work in a short space of time. The principal reason for people giving up on their needlepoints and becoming totally disenchanted is the length of time they believe is required to finish them. In fact with 10 holes per inch you can achieve a surprising amount of detail fairly quickly. Once you are proficient in tent stitch, even a cushion measuring 16" by 16" can be completed in ten days; using long stitch it can be done in half that time.

The HOLLYHOCK SCREEN

The Hollyhock screen is something that I longed to design for decades, and some years ago I spent an entire summer painting nothing but these flowers. Hollyhocks have always been high on my list of favorites and I was fur-

Howard Rice/GPL

ther determined by seeing them growing wild everywhere during the four years I lived in Yugoslavia.

Since double varieties have become more popular it can be difficult to find the lovely, single, old-fashioned hollyhocks. Having failed to grow my own, however, I found ample inspiration from the work of the Ukrainian folk artist Katerina Bilokur (1900–1961). Her writings describe eloquently the deep longings for expression in art that flowers engender. "You may not like my work as I paint only flowers. But how can I not paint them if they are so beautiful! ... When spring comes around and the fields turn green, and flowers begin to bloom, each prettier than the others ... My God, I forget everything, and again take to painting flowers."

As references I also used seed packets and photographs from magazines. You

will see from my sketches (right; below) that although I stuck fairly closely to the original shapes of the flowers drawn, as I worked I did alter the colors, and also changed the background. When stitching a piece, it is essential to keep pinning it up and looking at it, to see how it looks from a distance. This also makes the work more fun and carries the creative process into the stitching.

To make your own Hollyhock screen you can, if you prefer, work to a smaller scale. In any event the principles described above still apply. Having found good reference material I think it important to spend sufficient time at the drawing stage, so that you avoid the error so easily made of being too eager to start putting wool on canvas before the design is adequately resolved. Much time is saved in the long run by taking extra pains with the drawing and the tracing onto canvas. You can then decide on your color range and start stitching. In the case of my own Hollyhock tapestry it wasn't difficult to find someone willing and able to make a frame for the screen that rendered the finished work quite stunning and unusual.

Materials for the Hollyhock Screen

CANVAS:

3 pieces, gauge 7.6 holes per inch; each piece to measure 22" x 62" which allows 2" for stretching. Actual size of work: 18" x 58".

PATERNA YARNS were used for this screen, in the following colors:

Sky: Federal Blue 503, 504, 505

Clouds: White/Cream 260, 262, Dolphin D392, Grape 314, Ice Blue 556

Purple hills: Basil D117, D127, D137

Trees: Teal Blue 520, 521, 522

Greens: Hunter Green 612, 613, 615, Pine Green 662, 664, Loden Green 690, 691, 692, 693, 694, 695, Old Gold 755, Olive Green 654, Daffodil 763

Pinks: American Beauty 900, 902, 904, 905, Dusty Pink 914, Plum 326

Yellows: Daffodil 760, 762, 763, 764

Peaches: Salmon 840, 843, 844, 845, 846

Oranges: Woodrose 920, Butterscotch 703, 704, Copper 861, Ginger 883, Autumn Yellow 724

Background: Black/Charcoal 221, Coffee Brown 421, Donkey Brown D115, Pine Green 660, Forest Green 600

Once the pieces have been stitched, they need to be stretched out to their original size before being placed in the screen. The canvas can then be laced around the screen's plywood fillers, and backing material either glued or stitched into place.

With auriculae as with hollyhocks I prefer the fairly common single variety, in this case because of the blush of intense color around the pale center. To transform the newer hybrid varieties into needlepoint would certainly take some working at, since the colors of their flowers are almost surreal. Auriculae raised for showing are traditionally grown in earthenware pots; I like the fact that, in contrast to plastic containers, the pots themselves become an interesting color, from the lichen growing on them. With the pale auricula, the Sirius, a green Victorian-style jardiniere looked more fitting.

There is no reason why, as throughout the book, you shouldn't alter parts of this chart to suit your own tastes, substituting different fore- and backgrounds that appeal to you. It is fun for example to experiment with different colorways, to see how these affect the look of the plant itself.

The S I R I U S
A U R I C U L A
C U S H I O N

Sirius was a difficult variety of auricula to portray in yarn; nonetheless the shades used come fairly close. The background was inspired by one of Kaffe Fassett's knitted throws. I don't feel I'm just copying, in using other people's works as inspiration, because the result is so different from the original. This is partly due to my interpretation, and partly through the difference of the medium into which they are translated. A difference in scale between the reference and the piece inspired by it emphasizes this.

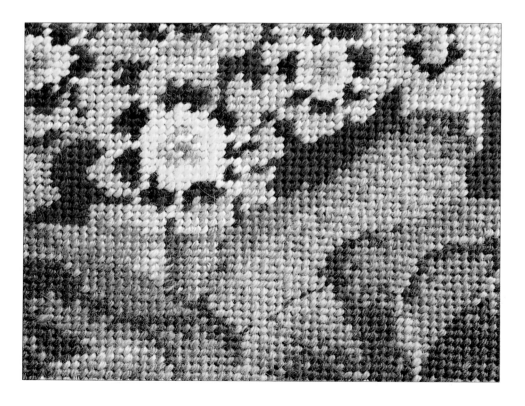

I raised auriculae from seed which were lovely enough to be an inspiration; they then failed to serve as a reference because of their short life span. Instead I used photographs from an excellent book by Brenda Hyatt (see p. 159). As you will see, the work changed quite a lot between the sketch and the finished piece. It makes an attractive companion to the auricula cushion in the next design.

Materials for the Sirius Cushion

CANVAS:

gauge 10 holes per inch; measuring 20" x 20"
which allows 2" for stretching.
Actual size of work: 16" x 16".

PATERNA YARNS:

Black/Charcoal 221, Blue Spruce 530,
Teal Blue 520, Ocean Green D516,
Loden Green 690, 692, 693,
Lime Green 670, Seafarer D503,
Pine Green 665, Federal Blue 500, 501,
Plum 320, 321, Fuchsia 354,
Antique Rose D281, Flesh 494,
Tobacco 743, 745, Daffodil 762,
White/Cream 262.

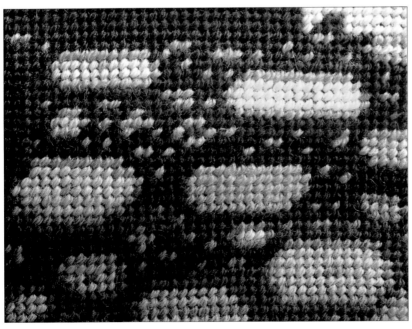

My own preference with subjects like this is to work the flowers and leaves first; then the vase, leaving the foreground and background till later as I may want to modify them. Once the stitching is finished, the piece will need stretching back to its original proportions before being made up into a cushion (see pp. 156–7).

The DARK AURICULA CUSHION

The originals for this I grew myself; in addition I found similar photographs, which showed the variety Alicia. An obscure Japanese stencil design was the source for the background. This fascinated me because although the stencil repeated, it was not obvious how it did so. The foreground was loosely based on a beautiful piece of textile which probably came from a kimono.

Sunniva Harte/GPL

It is interesting to see how the two finished cushions differ, even though the
subjects themselves are the same.

Materials for the
Dark Auricula Cushion

CANVAS:

gauge 10 holes per inch; measuring 20" x 20"
which allows a 2" border for stretching (pp.
156-7). Actual size of work: 16" x 16".

PATERNA YARNS:

Navy Blue 571, Black/Charcoal 221,
Periwinkle 341, 342, 343, Daffodil 762,
Lime Green 670, Loden Green 690, 692,
693, Fuschia 351, 353, Plum 320, 321,
Cinnamon D411, D419, Rust 870, Ocean
Green D516.

KEY

	Paterna
◤	571
╱	221
A	341
B	342
C	343
←	762
•	670
E	690
△	693
■	692
↘	351
◹	353
♥	320
→	D411
↑	D419
□	870
+	321
■	D516

Photocopy chart x 164% for actual size of tapestry

GARDENS

The challenge of flowers stitched en masse is irresistible to me; so too the remarkable range of styles in which gardens have been portrayed. Whether stitched as a tapestry or embroidered, the depiction of gardens has been popular for centuries, as a subject eclipsing even individual plants and flowers.

———————

Formal gardens, as in the large early eighteenth-century hangings now held at Montacute House in Somerset, have often been a subject in needlepoint. These tapestries, worked in fine tent stitch, combine an almost modern rendering of plant life with animals, birds and costumed figures that are quintessentially of their own period. The illustration on p. 34 shows the smaller of the panels comprising the hangings, in which a wealth of detail extends even to a servant tripping up in the foreground and spilling the contents of his tray. The hangings were housed originally at Stoke Edith, in Herefordshire, where they were made; unfortunately Stoke Edith House was destroyed by fire in 1927.

The Stoke Edith Tapestry at Montacute, Somerset, depicting a garden laid out in the formal style of the late seventeenth century.

Garden books make up much of my library of source material; sometimes, looking through these, I am struck by a photograph which sparks off a theme for a new work. One such was a picture of the garden at Nymans in West Sussex. For some time I had been thinking it would be fun to do a much bigger garden tapestry than I'd tried before. I wanted

National Trust Photographic Library

Clive Nichols

the foreground to be almost a field of different perennials, and in the background, formal gardens, fountains and statues, water gardens and follies. The picture of Nymans suggested just the right formal setting although it didn't have all the ingredients; I contented myself with just the fountain and the formal gardens for

Cabbages and chard in the formal potager at the Château de Villandry, France.

this hanging. It also intrigued me that the scene in the photograph, known as the secret garden, retains its air of mystery even when stitched in the tapestry. It is in fact a walled garden, but its walls are hidden, on one side by clematis and roses, on the other by shrubs and trees.

The IRISES *and* DELPHINIUMS HANGING

This piece came into being simply because I have always loved these flowers, both for their intense violet-blue colors and for the rich gold of the irises. They make a wonderfully joyous fore-

Topiary and fountain in the walled garden at Nymans, West Sussex

ground in contrast to the more somber scene behind, in which you can just see the four great topiary yews marking the center of the walled garden. The focus of the garden is an impressive Italian

National Trust Photographic Library/Ian Shaw

marble fountain, creating the appearance almost of a Renaissance setting.

———————

When I had finished the line drawing of the irises and delphiniums, I was pleased with how alive and almost dancing the sketch looked. You always hope this quality will carry through into the stitching itself, but you can never be quite sure until the work is completed. I feel it real-

ly has succeeded in this piece, which is intended as a glorious celebration of a garden in flower.

———————

Rather than follow the chart, some of you might want to stitch your own garden. Have a good look at all the areas of your garden, then make a few quick sketches, before you decide which parts you want to show. It is invaluable to take some photographs to work from, as inevitably the scene you choose will have changed before you finish stitching.

_____

You may also find it useful, during stitching as well as when creating the design, to make notes and sketches of any ideas that come to you for other needlepoints. The act of creativity often seems to have a spin-off effect, so that I find other possibilities keep occurring to me. I try to keep a diary of these, and sometimes a quick drawing too; it's surprising otherwise how quickly you forget your own best ideas.

In sketching from life, feel free to rearrange what you see. You may be inclined to stitch your rockery, herbaceous border and lily pond as parts of the same composition even though they aren't in the same area of the garden. Do drawings of each; take photographs; then do a rough sketch arranging them together as you would like them to be in your needlepoint.

_____

We often limit ourselves by trying to stay exactly true to life; but with our designs we have the artist's ultimate freedom of being able to show things precisely as we would like them to be. Mistakenly my children sometimes complain that their own drawings aren't "right." In answer I show them ancient Egyptian and Indian pictures, or European so-called naive paintings, to demonstrate that in art there are no such things as right or wrong, but only what the artist seeks to create, in any way that he or she wishes.

John Glover/GPL

Materials for the Irises and Delphiniums Hanging

CANVAS:

gauge 7.6 holes per inch; measuring 34" x 40", which allows a 2" border for stretching. Actual size of work: 30" x 36".

PATERNA YARNS:

White/Cream 261, Lavender 330, 331, 332, 334, Glacier 564, Pearl Grey 211, Periwinkle 340, 341, 342, Cobalt Blue 540, Violet 300, Old Blue 511, Blue Spruce 531, Ocean Green D516, Loden Green 691, Hunter Green 612, 613, Pine Green 663, 665, Lime Green 670, Mustard 712, Sunny Yellow 770, Marigold 800, Salmon 843, Old Gold 753, Tobacco 745, Plum 320.

The Irises and Delphiniums hanging is worked in random long stitch, which is one of the simplest and most versatile stitches. It is a variation on Gobelin stitch and is worked vertically over however many threads you wish - though ideally not more than four or five, otherwise the piece becomes loopy and unattractive and will not be so durable.

With this hanging you can start wherever you wish. My personal preference is to give in to the temptation of getting in the irises and delphiniums first and then move on to the formal garden in the background.

Once the stitching is finished, the work will require stretching. This is much easier however than with work done in tent stitch since the canvas will not have been pulled askew by a diagonal stitch.

The hanging can then simply be backed, leaving an opening at the top. Through this a rod can be run from which to suspend it. Alternatively, it can be framed in a complementary fabric, still with an opening for the rod in the backing material.

The VIEW *from a* WINDOW

The View from a Window pillow is more stylized than the Irises and Delphiniums hanging. Depending on how much time you want to spend, it could be done either to the size given here or, even more effectively, on a larger scale. It too is in random long stitch

The herb garden at Cranbourne Manor, Dorset.

which means you can fairly race along with the work.

———————

I had the idea for this needlepoint when looking out of the beautiful old stone windows of a friend's house. Her garden was not as formal as the one I've depicted but the color of the stone frame was so soft by comparison, I liked the idea of a fairly structured view. I would have liked to find windows with actual lichens and molds growing on them, but it seems people prefer the insides of their houses clean and mold free. Another feature of the work that appeals to me is the three cushions shown on the window seat. Though not precisely a trompe l'oeil, the idea of stitching a cushion with the likeness of stitched cushions is a gentle joke.

———————

The details of the view beyond the window were based on a picture of the herb garden, bordered with box hedges, at

Clay Perry

Cranbourne Manor in Dorset. In a piece of this size there isn't enough canvas space to do the original view full justice, but the work itself shows a pleasing mixture of garden and stonework. The range as well as the number of old gardens in Britain is marvelous, from the intricacies of this scene from Cranbourne to the broad vista of rhododendrons and lake that surrounds a grand house such as Sheffield Park in Sussex. If you decided to do needlepoint pieces of nothing but these, it would still be impossible to exhaust your sources of inspiration.

Materials for the View from a Window

CANVAS:

gauge size 10; measuring 28" x 22" (71 x 56cm) which allows a 2" (5cm) surround for stretching. Actual size of work: 24" x 18" (61 x 45.5cm).

PATERNA YARNS:

Old Blue 515, Dolphin D389, Steel Grey 201, Hunter Green 612, Pine Green 660, 662, Ocean Green D516, Blue Spruce 530, Loden Green 690, 691, 692, 693, 694, Olive Green 653, 654, Khaki Green 641, 643, 644, Forest Green 604, Honey Gold 733, Chocolate Brown 433, Beige Brown 462, Strawberry 950, American Beauty 904, Bittersweet 833, Spice 855, Mustard 710, Lavender 332, Federal Blue 501, 504, Periwinkle 342, Copper 862.

The order in which you stitch this depends on whether or not you like to start with the easier parts. I prefer to work the garden first, then the cushions followed by the stone window-surround, so that having done the complicated parts I know the rest of the work is just going to be relaxing.

Once stitched the work needs stretching out to its original size. As an alternative to being made up into a pillow or cushion it can also be fashioned as a small hanging or picture (see p. 157).

KEY

	Paterna
＼	515
⊥	D389
□	201
⊞	612
▶	660
И	662
▽	D516
⬟	530
△	690
6	691
H	692
//	693
⇖	694
L	653
↑	654
R	641
▪▪	643
⬠	644
∃	604
⊓	733
▬	433
⊐	462
K	950
▼	904
P	833
◤	855
✕	710
◇	332
●	501
✳	504
5	862
⊖	342

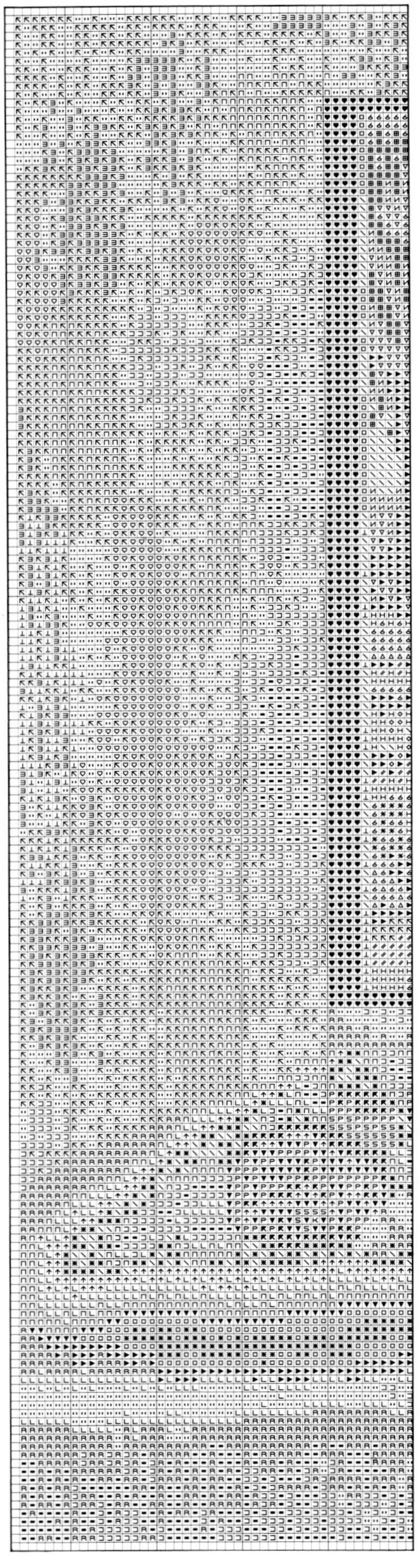

Photocopy chart x 218% for actual size of tapestry

L A N D S C A P E S

In this century, landscapes seem to have been neglected as a subject for needlepoint. Enchanting scenes have been portrayed previously, from at least as far back as the sixteenth century. Many different styles were used, even in the same period; some naturalistic, others charmingly naive. In the main the landscape was incidental to some other,

principal subject. It would often be executed nonetheless with great attention to detail, as in the cushion cover worked by Bess of Hardwick which shows the death of Actaeon. Here, natural features such as rocks, trees and water are delightfully stylized, even the bulrushes growing beside the water. Similarly prolific in its detail is the embroidered front

of a mid-eighteenth-century wing chair from Arniston House, in Lothian. A hay-making scene features a woman gathering hay, a man scything and another man talking to them both. On the horizon stands a horse and hay wagon, and the foreground is exuberant with exquisitely rendered meadow plants.

———————

In recent times people have lacked both the leisure and the inclination to attempt large hangings; most needlepoints have been made for small useful objects like cushions. Of course, as the two following projects show, not all landscapes have to

be done on a huge scale. But as you gain in experience and confidence there is no reason to forgo the pleasure of stitching a large wall hanging.

———————

The two landscapes in this section were conceived and worked as a complementary pair. The idea was to represent two completely different types of atmosphere: a lush English countryside, and the rich, sun-drenched tones of autumnal Tuscany. My own mind's-eye view of England is pastoral and sees a stream flowing through a meadow against a background of trees and rolling hills. It stems from memories of childhood and long hot summer days in Somerset when, in my mind at least, the sun always seemed to be shining and the sky was incredibly blue. By contrast with the greenness of rural England I wanted the Tuscan landscape to have more vibrant golds and earth tones, with cypress trees, fields of sunflowers and rows of vines.

To interpret each of these I first set out to show the look of a particular landscape. It had occurred to me that a pastoral scene on its own wouldn't quite be enough as a subject for a needlepoint piece. So I also wanted to evoke the spirit of the country, using a border of fruits and flowers to offset the actual landscape to best advantage.

For reference I was able to find photographs of landscapes that readily conveyed the atmosphere I wanted to re-create. As for the border details, when I think of Mediterranean countries what comes to me first is the smell of ripe fruits, and cypresses in baking heat, and the warm taste of grapes plucked straight from the vine. So it seemed just right to give the Tuscan landscape a border of grapes, vine leaves, sunflowers and a pumpkin. For the English piece, I wanted a border made up of full, overblown late-season garden flowers. When I came to look for references, it seems strange in

view of the subject that I found the best among the Dutch painters of the seventeenth century, the atmosphere and definition of whose canvases perfectly convey the almost iridescent quality of the flowers.

The ENGLISH LANDSCAPE

Materials for the English Landscape

CANVAS:

gauge 10 holes per inch; measuring 21" x 27", which allows a 2" border for stretching. Actual size of work: 17" x 23".

PATERNA YARNS:

Pine Green 660, Loden Green 690, 691, 692, 693, 694, Hunter Green 612, 613, Olive Green 651, 652, 654, Khaki Green 643, 644, Honey Gold 733, Autumn Yellow 725, Butterscotch 703, American Beauty 900, 902, 904, 905, Hot Pink 964,
Cobalt Blue 540, Periwinkle 340, 341, 342, 343, Pearl Grey 211, 212, Steel Grey 201, Cream/White 262.

I suggest that when working these two pictures you start by stitching the borders. The whole work is much easier if you first get good sharp outlines for the shapes within each border, then stitch the landscape and finally work the colors between the surrounding leaves and flowers and the edge of the landscape.

Once the work is stitched it requires stretching back to its original dimensions. It can then be made up into a hanging

either simply by backing it with a suitable fabric and leaving a space at the top through which to slide a thin rod from which it can be hung, or by framing it with another fabric and backing it in such a way that a rod can be passed through spaces at the topmost corners (see p. 157).

The TUSCAN LANDSCAPE

Materials for the Tuscan Landscape

CANVAS:

gauge 10 holes per inch; measuring 21" x 27", which allows a 2" border for stretching. Actual size of work: 17" x 23".

PATERNA YARNS:

Charcoal 221, Teal Blue 520, 521, Seafarer D501, Loden Green 691, 693, Olive Green 652, Khaki Green 641, Earth Brown 410, 413, Chocolate Brown 432, Autumn Yellow 720, 723, 725, Ginger 883, Old Gold 755, Mustard 710, 712, Hunter Green 613, Pearl Grey 210, Periwinkle 342, 343, 344, Cobalt Blue 543, 544, 545, Pine Green 662, American Beauty 900, Cranberry 940, Christmas Red 970.

Just as for the English Landscape, once the work is stitched it needs stretching, and making up as a hanging, with or without framing it in another fabric before backing it and leaving room to put a thin rod through the top of the piece.

KEY

Paterna

▼	221		▪▪	710
●❘●	520		⊖	712
☐	521		⊒	613
⊞	D501		◢	210
↓	691		✳	342
←	693		⊐	343
▽	652		⅃	344
▼	641		❘	344
◤	410		/	543
▽	413		\	544
◀	432		—	545
∥	723		♥	662
◸	725		▲	900
■	720		●	940
↑	883		人	970
∧	755			

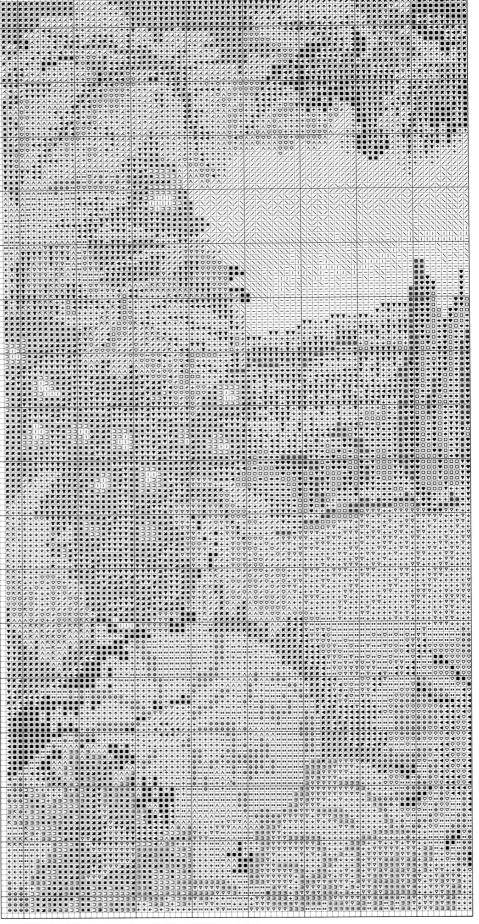

Photocopy chart x 170% for actual size of tapestry

W A T E R

When I first thought about depicting water in stitching and started looking at source material, I soon realized that this too was a subject you could pursue for the rest of your life without any risk of becoming jaded. When asked how on earth I get design ideas, I am surprised that people think this difficult. Nature is a big enough subject in itself, and it expands to include the ways in which people have seen it and made designs, both directly and by abstracting its forms and spaces.

If ever you lack ideas, take a walk and really try to observe what you are looking at. As we grow older we take so much for granted, so that often we don't notice things as accurately as we think. We have got too used to the world to see it in its true beauty as we did when we were young. But if you remember this, and put an effort into observing nature afresh, ideas will start to form almost before your very eyes. Your only problem will then be the preferable one of finding time to put so many possibilities onto paper and canvas.

———————

Water, like other subjects, can be stitched either in a stylized way or naturalistically. Both have their own charm and fascination, whether used to represent lily ponds, water gardens, seascapes, or waterfalls in a jungle for example, framed by orchids and other exotic plants.

———————

Having got the confidence to act on your own ideas you will find that, in depicting

Opposite:
The cascade and
grotto at Bowood
House, Wiltshire.

water, as with other subjects one design usually leads to another. While stitching, you may feel you could have interpreted the subject better. But instead of unpicking and trying again, you would do best to keep a notebook recording ways of stitching certain parts more effectively another time, along with any new designs that spring to mind. You cannot tell what needs to be altered in a piece before it is finished; stitching things in only to take them out is therefore doubly a waste of time. One of the fascinations of needlepoint is that, though some part you have stitched may seem not quite right, once the surrounding material is completed, the same area more often than not will look just as you wanted. When I was working with Kaffe Fassett this was something he told me over and over again, and it has stood me in very good stead.

Clay Perry/GPL

The WATERFALLS HANGING

In this piece I wanted to see if it was actually possible to stitch the water dripping and falling over mossy rocks. It was inspired by Capability Brown's waterfall at Bowood in Wiltshire. Gainsborough, the English painter, was commissioned by Lord Shelburne in 1767 to paint three pictures for Bowood that were intended to lay the foundation of British landscape. Capability Brown finished his contribution to Bowood in 1768; but the cascade was subsequently altered, by Charles Hamilton in 1785, in order for it to look more like a painting by Poussin.

––––––––––

With so much trouble taken to achieve a painterly effect in real life, it was strange to find myself changing this waterfall yet again, this time as a subject to be stitched as a needlepoint hanging. To make the design concentrated I placed the falls slightly closer together than they actually are; I also stitched the piece with more water than usual flowing over the rocks.

This was a challenging and fascinating subject. It confirmed for me that you cannot tell how dark or light a yarn is going to look until it is stitched in place next to another color, as each yarn used for the water seemed almost white until placed by the adjacent one, when their colors showed surprisingly strongly. Almost the entire piece was done on faith because only towards finishing it could I see that the water actually would look like water.

––––––––––

To make your own waterfalls hanging, follow the procedure of making sketches from life or from good photographs, then decide what size piece you want to do and make a line drawing to scale. Finally, ink in the outlines and transfer them to the canvas. I found it useful when working this piece to give the outline a color wash. With other subjects I don't always bother to do this, as I much prefer to work out the colors as I

stitch. But most of this hanging is worked in yarns that are very close in tone, so that in addition to consulting photographs I found such a sketch invaluable as a reference.

———————————

Remember when working water to use much lighter colors than seem necessary—once yarn is stitched onto the canvas, it tends to look slightly darker than

you anticipate. Lots of brilliant white and off-white, and the very palest shades of blue, green and even lavender—you have to experiment. Even the shadows between water are quite pale.

Materials for the Waterfalls Hanging

CANVAS:

gauge 10 holes per inch; measuring 34" x 34", which allows a 2" border for stretching. Actual size of work: 30" x 30".

PATERNA YARNS:

Forest Green 601, 602, Olive Green 650, 652, 653, Loden Green 690, 691, 692, 693, Pine Green 660, 664, Blue Spruce 531, Teal Blue 520, Tobacco 743, Steel Grey 204, Grape 314, Ocean Green D527, White/Cream 260, 261, Dolphin D392.

Once the piece is stitched it should be stretched to its original dimensions and backed or framed (see p. 157).

The ANGEL FISH *and the* SQUIRREL FISH

The Angel Fish and Squirrel Fish cushions were inspired by the extremely beautiful photography in Vic Cox's Ocean Life: Beneath the Crystal Seas (see p. 159). I loved the shining bodies of the fish, the luminous quality of aquamarine sea with sunlight filtering through, and the reefs of coral which in themselves seemed like a tapestry. Was it possible, I wondered, to convey this depth and color in needlepoint, and the sense of being underwater? I feel now that this can be done very successfully, and I've gained many more ideas for aquatic designs.

Materials for the Angel Fish Cushion

CANVAS:

gauge 10 holes per inch; measuring 21" x 21", which allows a 2" border for stretching. Actual size of work: 17" x 17".

PATERNA YARNS:

White/Cream 260, Pearl Grey 213, Dolphin D346, D389, Charcoal/Black 221, Sky Blue 580, 581, 583, 585, Teal Blue 522, Federal Blue 500, Dusty Pink 913, Woodrose 922, Donkey Brown D115, Chocolate Brown 432, Copper 863, Grape 313, Beige Brown 461.

The Angel Fish cushion is worked in
tent stitch. It needs stretching to its
original dimensions once stitched, and
can then be made up into a cushion
(see p. 157).

	Paterna
A	260
B	213
C	D389
D	D346
■	221
/	580
		581
▽	583
⠒	585
→	522
●	500
//	913
↖	922
◇	D115
✳	432
V	863
▪▪	313
▽	461

Photocopy chart x 195% for actual size of tapestry

Squirrel Fish, Pterois sp.; Plate 33. Zoological drawing by Ferdinand Bauer (1760-1826).

The Squirrel fish, though a similar subject, has an entirely different quality about it, not only because of its glowing golden-orange colors as opposed to the severe stripes of the Angel fish but because it has a more mysterious underwater look. Nevertheless the two pieces form handsome complementary designs.

KEY

	Paterna						
↑	262	И	652	◻	862	⊓	211
◀	221	5	642	H	842	∧	580
2	660	←	644	E	843	T	581
◤	661	⋏	745	✎	844	L	582
▽	D516	+	732	⠿	845	Y	583
⊐	601	V	870	9	885	=	584
1	604	■	D411	◼	500	◤	592
＼	521	B	720	◇	505	⋊	593
		W	852	P	510	▼	400

Photocopy chart x 195% for actual size of tapestry

Materials for the Squirrel Fish Cushion

CANVAS:

gauge 10 holes per inch; measuring
21" x 21", which allows a 2" border for
stretching. Actual size of work: 17" x 17".

PATERNA YARNS:

White/Cream 262, Black/Charcoal 221,
Pine Green 660, 661, Ocean Green D516,
Forest Green 601, 604, Teal Blue 521,
Olive Green 652, Khaki Green 642, 644,
Tobacco 745, Honey Gold 732, Rust 870,
Cinnamon D411, Autumn Yellow 720,
Spice 852, Copper 862, Salmon 842, 843,
844, 845, Ginger 885, Federal Blue 500,
505, Old Blue 510, Pearl Grey 211, Sky
Blue 580, 581, 582, 583, 584, Caribbean
Blue 592, 593, Fawn Brown 400.

The Squirrel Fish cushion is also worked
in tent stitch and needs stretching after
being stitched, before being made up
into a cushion (see p. 157).

P A T T E R N S

I have always been fascinated by patterns, and have used them many times in needlepoints as a background, even though taken on their own they have never been my forte. I have enjoyed working with repeat patterns when designing wallpapers and fabrics; for needlepoints however I prefer to work directly from different sources and let the piece evolve as I stitch it onto the canvas. Patterns for needlepoint tend to be better when worked out first on graph paper, or at least roughly sketched, before being experimentally colored in. I have included this chapter just to show that in tapestry a very simple pattern can be surprisingly effective, as you will see from the Heraldic cushion (p. 87).

Of all the sources for patterning in needlepoint, one of the most attractive is tile designs. Using only a basic pattern, a multitude of combinations becomes possible, especially when you vary the colors. You can get an idea of this from the designs shown here and on p. 83. With some the effect just depends on whether you are looking at the darker areas primarily and the lighter parts secondarily, or vice versa.

Tiles in the Topkapi Palace, Istanbul.

Decorative tile-making is thought by many to have reached its finest form in the art of Islam, with such achievements as the awe-inspiring dome at the entrance to the Royal Mosque in Isfahan. Nearer the geographical limits of the medieval Muslim world are the marvellous designs in the Alhambra Palace in Granada, part of a long Spanish tradition of accomplished work in tiles, associated with the Moorish influence.

Francesco Venturi/KEA

Francesco Venturi/KEA

The HERALDIC CUSHION

The idea for this cushion was loosely based on a seventeenth-century "diamond point" pattern, which in turn had derived from a number of late sixteenth-century designs from Seville. Some elements I chose with a view to making a repeating cushion design; to give this a deeper perspective I then used different shades of blue, red and gold. Not only does this make the result more interesting, but the cushion is more fun to stitch.

KEY

Paterna

○	900
△	902
Ε	903
△	341
✳	342
/	540
⬠	711
✕	713
+	731

Materials for the Heraldic Cushion

CANVAS:

*gauge 7.6 holes per inch; measuring
26" x 26", which allows a 2" border for
stretching. Actual size of work: 22" x 22".*

PATERNA YARNS:

*American Beauty 900, 902, 903,
Periwinkle 341, 342, Cobalt 540,
Mustard 711, 713, Honey Gold 731.*

This piece is worked in tent stitch, after which it should be stretched to its original dimensions and shape. It can then be made into a cushion, with tassels attached at the corners. Originally I thought it might look splendid as a table carpet, which was a furnishing much used by the Victorians; but a cushion would probably be more in keeping with modern tastes.

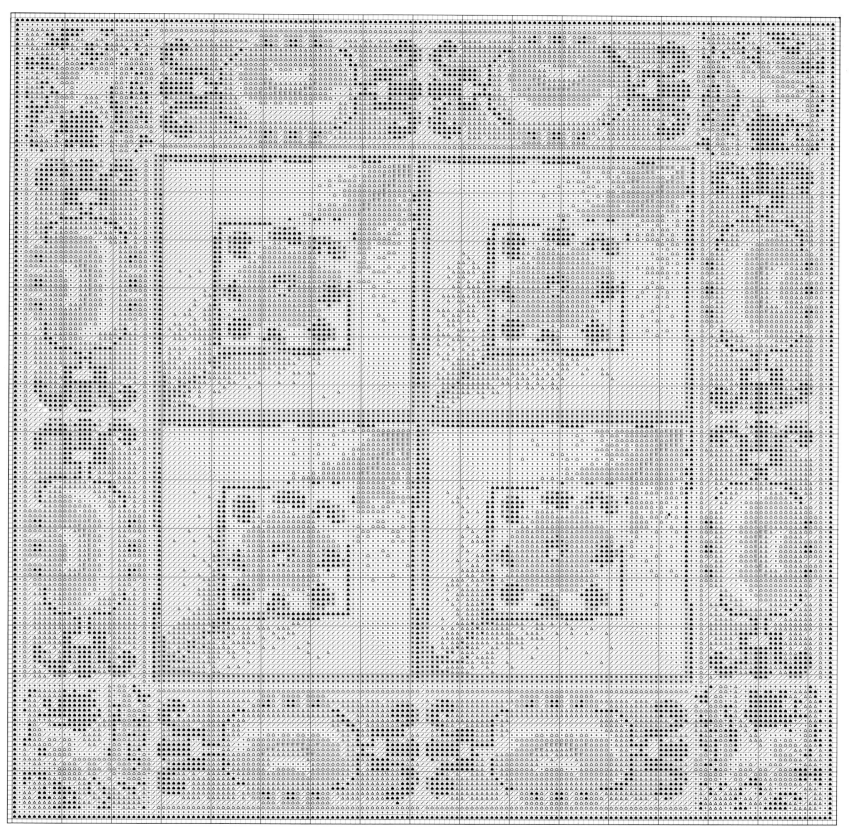

Photocopy chart x 252% for actual size of tapestry

Francesco Venturi/KEA

The STAR TILE PLACEMATS

These mats are worked in two totally dissimilar colorways, to show how the choice and placement of colors can change a simple design. An important inspiration for them was the Islamic or

Opposite:
Tiles in the Hazrat
Hizir Mosque,
Samarkand,
Uzbekistan.

Ottoman Star, which since the thirteenth century has been given many decorative forms. Using different colorways, it would be possible to achieve a complete set of contrasting placemats. Start by

making a rough drawing and coloring it, remembering that it is much quicker to re-draw or re-paint a design than to stitch part of it again. When I stitched the paler colorway it was not until the work was well advanced that I realized stronger colors were needed and a large part would have to be restitched.

Materials for Placemat One

CANVAS:

gauge 10 holes per inch; measuring 15" x 21", which allows a 2" border for stretching. Actual size of work: 11" x 17".

PATERNA YARNS:

Cobalt 540, Sky Blue 581, 583, Strawberry 950, White 260, Old Gold 755, Navy Blue 571.

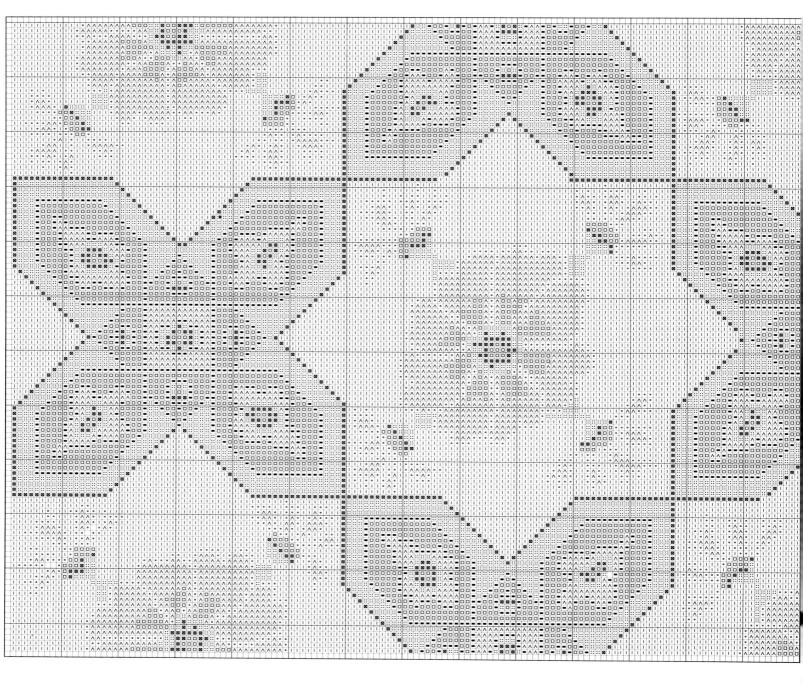

KEY

	Paterna			
|	540	□	950	
⊠	583	o	260	
⫶	581	∧	755	
		▬	571	

KEY

	Paterna			
|	751	□	874	
⊠	851	o	494	
⫶	863	∧	693	
		▬	694	

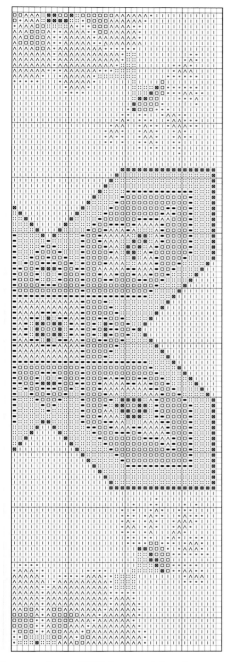

Materials for Placemat Two

CANVAS:

gauge 10 holes per inch; measuring 15" x 21", which allows a 2" border for stretching. Actual size of work: 11" x 17".

PATERNA YARNS:

Old Gold 751, Spice 851, Copper 863, Rust 874, Flesh 494, Loden Green 693, 694.

Once stitched, the placemats need stretching back to their original dimensions and shape. They can then be backed with a non-slip fabric. So that they do not absorb food spillages and become stained, they can either be treated with a spray or mounted in Plexiglas frames. If you use a spray, test it first on a scrap piece of work to make sure it will not discolor the work.

BEAUTIFUL
OBJECTS

The great treasure-house of London's Victoria and Albert Museum is to me the ultimate source of beautiful objects. Because of the diversity one finds there it is the place I love to go to more than anywhere in the city. The first time I visited the museum I could not believe the quantity and splendor of what there was to see. After nearly a day of wandering about making sketches its bombardment of the senses left me exhausted. It was at that point that I had the surprise of finding another level downstairs, housing artifacts from Tibet and Nepal. I spent the rest of the time there until the museum closed, overwhelmed by the things I discovered. Even now, just thinking about that day gives me the same sense of amazement that so many people down the centuries have made so many beautiful things.

———————————

Some artifacts displayed in the Victoria and Albert Museum depend for their

Skink, Egernia cunninghami; *Plate 27. Zoological drawing by Ferdinand Bauer (1760–1826).*

effect on presenting nature in an unusual way—often so that some creature becomes beautiful to us for the first time. One day while searching for reference material I came across a wonderful hand-colored engraving from Roesel von Rosenhof's Histoire Naturalis Ranarum (1758). I was so struck by its colors that I realized the fire salamander it depicted was a beautiful object in its own right. It

The Natural History Museum, London

reminded me of a time when I was travelling through France with my young son. We were on a camp site and he was digging in the earth, as children do, beneath a tree, when he shouted to me to come and look. What he had found at the bottom of his six-inch hole was a European fire salamander. It seemed almost incredible to have found this lurid little creature there. We were both so pleased—

but not quite sure if it was dangerous. Though later we found it was not poisonous, at the time we made haste to cover it up and leave it in peace.

———————

Having begun to look on such creatures as beautiful, I realized that hitherto I'd ignored a wealth of material. We are mostly used to the idea that, as subjects for needlepoint, flowers and butterflies,

Right:
Golden bell frog,
Litoria aurea; *Plate*
26. Zoological
drawing by
Ferdinand Bauer
(1760-1826).

The Natural History Museum, London

birds, landscapes and water scenes are all suitable. Many people would not have the same view of reptiles and amphibians; but when you begin to take notice of them, the elegance of their shapes and markings becomes clear to see.

The FROG *and* LIZARD RUNNER

Although our European fire salamander proved harmless, the other of nature's objets de vertu in this piece is extremely toxic to humans. As one of the poison arrow frogs of South America he is named for an obvious reason. I included him because his striking resemblance to the salamander colorwise made me think the runner would look interesting if it featured them both.

The simple but effective border was worked out after the runner itself was finished. Once the main stitching was completed it was easier to see whether this edging should complement it or offer a contrast.

Materials for the Frog and
Lizard Runner

———————

CANVAS:

    gauge 10 holes per inch; measuring
    13" x 28", which allows a 2" border for
    stretching. Actual size of work; 9" x 24".

PATERNA YARNS:

    Black/Charcoal 220, 221, Pine Green 660,
662, Loden Green 690, 691, Khaki Green
640, Olive Green 651, 652, 653, Verdigris
D511, Old Gold 751, Autumn Yellow 720,
Pearl Grey 210, 211, Steel Grey 201,
Butterscotch 700, Mustard 711, 712.

———————

Once stitched the runner can be stretched back to its original proportions and backed with a suitable non-slip material.

Michael Fogden

Warning coloration of the poison dart frog, Dendrobates leucomelas, *from the rain forests of Guyana and Venezuela.*

KEY

	Paterna		D511
●	660	G	751
↓	690	\	751
Ɛ	691	△	201
H	651	И	662
\\	652	+	720
◤	640	∧	700
		T	711

Photocopy chart x 146% for actual size of tapestry

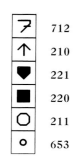

712	
210	
221	
220	
211	
653	

The V & A FLOWERS CUSHION

A plate in the Victoria and Albert Museum was the inspiration for this. It is Welsh and dates from between 1811 and 1819, and is elegantly painted with a basket of full-blown garden flowers. I loved the vibrant warmth of the blooms, but decided to leave out the basket. As a background to the bouquet I decided on a very pale brocade, which works effectively without introducing new colors. The border was suggested by a chair seat from the V & A's textile collection, dated 1737 and depicting a stylized vase of flowers. From it I fitted various elements around the bouquet, echoing its richness and making a good edge to the pale brocade.

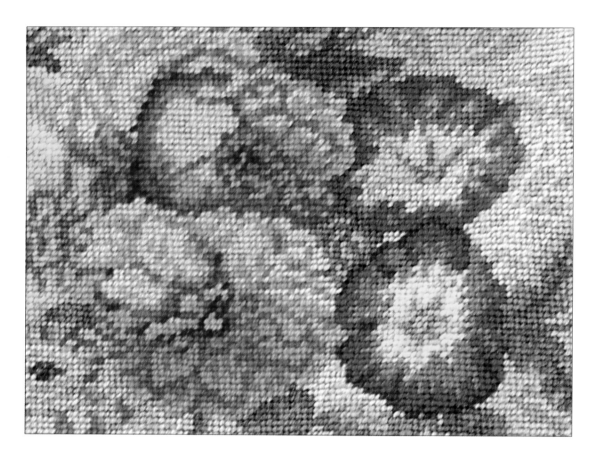

	Paterna
◤	D516
⌐	761
↓	711
▽	712
⧠	D521
◣	902
◥	904
∷	906
—	326
●	910
▬	612
△	613
←	653
▢	671
P	505
■	340
L	342
✕	256

Materials for the
V & A Flowers Cushion

CANVAS:

gauge size 10 ; measuring 23" x 23"
(58.5 x 58.5cm) which allows a 2" (5cm)
surround for stretching. Actual size of work:
19" x 19". (47.5 x 47.5cm)

PATERNA YARNS:

Ocean Green D516, Daffodil 761, Mustard
711, 712, Verdigris D521, American Beauty
902, 904, 906, Plum 326, Dusty Pink 910,
Hunter Green 612, 613, Olive Green 653,
Lime Green 671, Federal Blue 505,
Periwinkle 340, 342, Warm Grey 256.

Photocopy chart x 218% for actual size of tapestry

Once the piece is stitched it can be
stretched back to its original dimensions
and shape and made up into a cushion.

F R U I T

&

V E G E T A B L E S

These have been an acceptable subject over many centuries for still-life painters, but as subjects for decorative textiles they have not been widely adopted. Until recently this was partic-ularly so in modern times. Fruits and vegetables have been used as border details, and served as an occasional reference in hangings with a biblical subject, but generally there are few textiles

in any form that have illustrated them as a central subject.

———————————

Anyone who is familiar with the collections of the Victoria and Albert Museum will know just how widely fruit and vegetables have been used in ceramics, both as painted decoration and as part of the form of the objects themselves. One exceptional example that I particularly like is a cauliflower teapot in the Museum, because of its lovely off-white knobbly top and the frothy green, beautifully curled leaves surrounding it.

———————————

It was these glimpses of the variety of

design and texture to which everyday vegetables lend themselves, and from the pleasure I got from stitching different fruits and garden crops while working with Kaffe Fassett, that really got me excited about their enormous potential as tapestry subjects. And, of course, growing wonderful varieties of pumpkins, gourds and all manner of squash in Yugoslavia must have been quite an influence. These have the same appeal as nasturtiums for me – the fact that they creep over everything, forming exquisite patterns with their leaves, then brighten the garden with their beautiful golden flowers and finally produce their massive fruits.

Mayer/Le Scanff/GPL

The
PUMPKINS, FIGS
and MUSHROOMS
CUSHION

Starting with an overall idea of autumnal fruits, this piece had several sources. The pumpkins were mostly prompted by William Hammer's painting *Baskets of Fruit on the Steps of a Terrace* (1852) (see p. 121). The original picture

Pumpkins and squash stored on a greenhouse shelf.

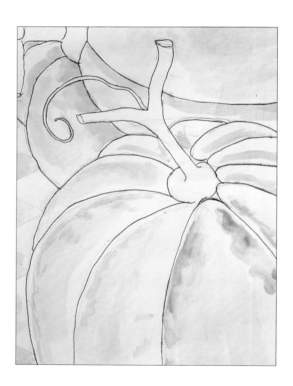

Mayer/Le Scanff/GPL

had many other details that would inspire translation into needlepoint; however the only other one I have used is the stone-tiled floor. You can see from my watercolor sketch that quite a lot changed between conception and finished work. The projected border of blackberries was put aside as being the wrong scale; also a stone-tiled background did not suit a similar floor, so the background was changed, throwing the pumpkins into relief.

Baskets of Fruit on the Steps of a Terrace *(1852), by William Hammer.*

The same artist also painted a still life of *Figs, Walnuts, an Orange and a Lemon,* from which I garnered ideas for the rest of my design.

Christie's, London

Materials for the Pumpkins, Figs and Mushrooms Cushion

CANVAS:

gauge 10 holes per inch; measuring 28" x 28", which allows a 2" border for stretching. Actual size of work: 24" x 24".

PATERNA YARNS:

White/Cream 261, Periwinkle 342, 344, Pearl Grey 212, Steel Grey 201, Pine Green 665, Hunter Green 612, 613, Loden Green 691, Ocean Green D516, Blue Spruce 531, American Beauty 900, Strawberry 950, Rusty Rose 931, Wood Rose 922, Old Gold 753, Autumn Yellow 725, Butterscotch 704, Marigold 800, Plum 320, 324, 325, Grape 311, 312, 313, Cinnamon D423.

This cushion is worked in random long stitch, which means that for a fairly large piece it doesn't take that long to complete.

Once the piece is stitched it should be stretched back to its original dimensions and shape and can then be made up into a large cushion (see p. 157).

The BLUE PLUM *and* RED FRUIT CUSHIONS

It was a chance viewing of a magazine cover that I caught sight of one day showing photographs of plums which inspired the Blue Plum cushion. The illustrations looked luscious, as did the fruit. Inside the magazine I found further sumptuous photography of the same kind, so much so that I was unable to decide on just one subject. Instead I designed a complementary piece, the Red Fruit cushion.

Little alteration would have been needed to translate any of the photographs into a one-off design. But in order to fashion two cushions as a complementary pair, it was necessary to rearrange the fruit and reduce the range of colors to within manageable bounds. Over the years you are apt to collect various bits and pieces of yarns and eventually you should have enough colors for the most complicated work. But until you have stitched enough needlepoints to have gathered a library of yarns it is very expensive to buy hundreds of colors just for one piece.

	Paterna
○	764
L	710
J	712
▬	833
▼	862
←	904
▽	301
И	311
△	913
◤	970
B	341
/	662
↖	664
→	612
↑	433
∵	334
I	221
▽	344

Old Venetian marble designs inspired both the backgrounds for these cushions; the foregrounds were taken from textile designs. You will see from the sketch for the Red Fruit cushion (p. 132) that when I came to do the actual stitching the colour sequence was altered. Once on canvas, it was clear that the design would work better that way round. It's fun to play around with foreground and background

Photocopy chart x 177% for actual size of tapestry

colors and try the effect of various changes. Unfortunately this can also be time-consuming, since it's hard to judge any part of your canvas until you've stitched quite a large area. On these designs I think the Red Fruit cushion's burnt cinnamon colors are especially effective in offsetting the fresh greens and deep luminous blues and violets of its companion piece.

Materials for the Blue Plum Cushion

CANVAS:

gauge 10 holes per inch;
measuring 19.5" x 19.5", which allows
2" for stretching.
Actual size of work: 15.5" x 15.5".

PATERNA YARNS:

Daffodil 764, Mustard 710, 712, Bittersweet 833, Copper 862, American Beauty 904, Violet 301, Grape 311, Dusty Pink 913, Christmas Red 970, Periwinkle 341, Pine Green 662, 664, Hunter Green 612, Chocolate Brown 433, Lavender 334, Charcoal 221, Periwinkle 344.

	Paterna
●	221
■	560
T	343
V	D281
Ⅎ	612
—	643
\	754
ϭ	263
△	722
+	725
/	727
●	D411
◤	862
↑	863
▶	950
▪▪	900

Materials for the Red Fruit Cushion

CANVAS:

gauge size 10; measuring 19.5" x 19.5" (49 x 49cm) which allows 2" (5cm) for stretching. Actual size of work: 15.5" x 15.5" (39.5 x 39.5cm).

PATERNA YARNS:

Black/Charcoal 221, Glacier 560, Periwinkle 343, Antique Rose D281, Hunter Green 612, Khaki Green 643, Old Gold 754, White/Cream 263, Autumn Yellow 722, 725, 727, Cinnamon D411, Copper 862, 863, Strawberry 950, American Beauty 900.

Photocopy chart x 177% for actual size of tapestry

Once the works have been stitched, they need to be stretched back to their original proportions and size. When making them up into cushions, use suitably rich backing fabrics to set off the colors of the stitching (see p. 157).

BIRDS

&

BUTTERFLIES

From its earliest history these have been favorite subjects for needlepoint. In the seventeenth century they were wrought into many kinds of furnishing fabrics whose artistry was exceptional.

One example is a pair of armchairs dated 1635, from the large suite in the Great Chamber at Hardwick in Derbyshire (p. 144). The beauty of using birds and butterflies on designs like these is that

James Hancock

Peacock butterfly.

they can be placed anywhere without being illogical.

_____

For this chapter my first idea was a hanging which would be panoramic enough to show a huge flock of birds taking off or a swarming mass of butterflies with opened wings. But whatever its attractiveness such a spectacle would have demanded a huge amount of time and thought; so I settled for the similar but less complex Flamingo panel.

_____

The idea for this came from the stylized posing of a group of flamingoes I saw while taking the children to the zoo. I was amused by the fact that at first glance you could not tell where the birds' lowered heads and resting legs were. Noting how monochromatic and mysterious they appeared as a group, I took some photographs to use for a reference. Standing as they were with masses of pampas grass bending over them, they had the simplicity of color and precise lines that I associate with Japanese art.

The FLAMINGO PANEL

Drawing the flamingoes proved diffi-cult for some reason—perhaps because I felt it important for each to be slightly different, as well as spacing them so that the overall effect was pleasing. With hindsight I can see many things I would have done another way—so I'm all the more glad to have made notes as I worked that I can use the next time.

Materials for the Flamingo Panel

CANVAS:

gauge 10 holes per inch; measuring 28" x 40", which allows a 2" border for stretching. Actual size of work: 24" x 36".

PATERNA YARNS:

Coffee Brown 420, White/Cream 260, 261, Pearl Grey 213, Dolphin D389, Olive Green 654, Khaki Green 644, Mustard 716, Tobacco 744, Forest Green 601, 602, 603, 604, 605, Pine Green 660, Bittersweet 830, 834, 835, Copper 862, Salmon 845, 846, Flesh 493, Terracotta 486, Rust 875.

It surprised me that twenty-three different yarns were needed for something whose coloring looks so simple.

Once the piece is stitched, stretch to its original proportions, and choose a suitable fabric to back the piece, with or without using a fabric to frame it.

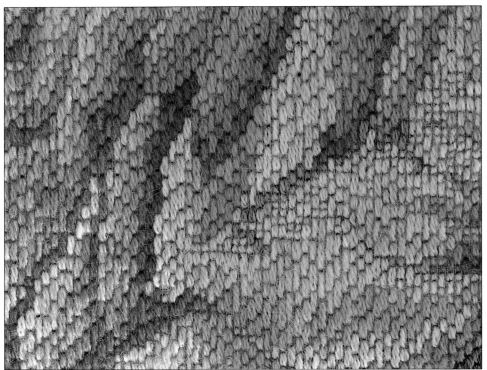

The BUTTERFLY FIRESCREEN

For a firescreen I thought a traditional arrangement would be popular. A nineteenth-century book illustration was my starting point but I varied the subjects by adding several different butterfly species from the British Isles.

———————

This piece is worked in tent stitch, which

Embroidery detail on a seventeenth-century chair in the High Great Chamber, Hardwick Hall, Derbyshire.

has been traditional for a firescreen, often being used with petit point for details such as figures and faces. Clockwise from the top, the butterflies illustrated are Large Heath, Duke of Burgundy Fritillary, Camberwell Beauty, Swallowtail, Red Admiral, and Little Peacock Butterfly. In reality they would

National Trust Photographic Library/Andrew Haslam

James Hancock

Comma polygonia
c. album *butterfly*.

KEY

	Paterna
∴	551
/	552
\	553
—	555
◤	902
⬞	950
◁	862
⊖	743
△	752
▬	731
L	720
∧	610
◸	611
→	612
↑	613
+	690
=	693
▽	694
⌂	421
B	451
C	452
D	441
I	261
▼	221

be unlikely to settle together onto the same plant, but some artistic licence is allowable. The plant is in fact a wild raspberry - though despite its height everyone who saw the piece while I was stitching it, seemed to think it was a strawberry.

To set off the butterflies and plant to best advantage I played around for some time with different backgrounds before I decided upon the vivid graded blue used here.

146

Photocopy chart x 175% for actual size of tapestry

Once worked the piece needs stretching back to its original dimensions and mounting in the firescreen. It is better to leave the wool exposed, as it tends to sweat and discolour if put behind glass or perspex.

Materials for the
Butterfly Firescreen

CANVAS:

gauge 10 holes per inch; measuring
23.5" x 19.5" which allows a 2" surround
for stretching. Actual size of work:
21.5" x 17.5". The screen frame itself is
supplied in centimetres, so the measurements
given here will not be exact.

PATERNA YARNS:

Ice Blue 551, 552, 553, 555,
American Beauty 902, Strawberry 950,
Copper 862, Tobacco 743, Old Gold 752,
Honey Gold 731, Autumn Yellow 720,
Hunter Green 610, 611, 612, 613,
Loden Green 690, 693, 694, Coffee Brown
421, Khaki Brown 451, 452,
Golden Brown 441, White/Cream 261.

The KINGFISHER HANGING

The final work in this section could equally well be made up into a cushion. What moved me to design it was the beauty of this lovely little bird which, though rarely glimpsed, epitomizes the English riverside. To catch sight of a kingfisher is the more wonderful in that its vivid colors evoke a tropical rainforest, so unexpected in our more temperate climate.

If this work is used as a cushion, a border will be needed because much of the picture would otherwise be lost in the curve of the cushion.

Long stitch is used on this piece, to echo the design's painterly quality. However, it could equally well be worked using each square of color as one tent stitch.

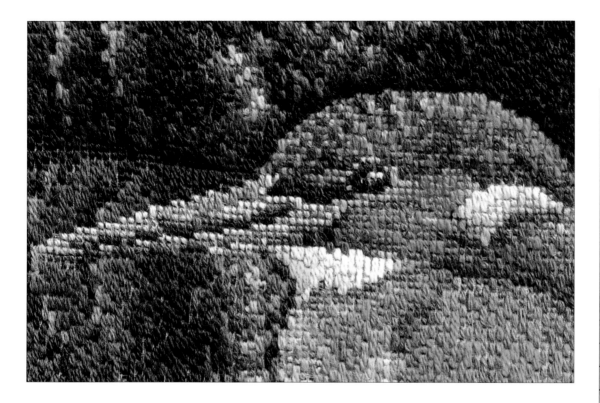

KEY

	Paterna
◦	221
∨	D346
⬟	D389
⋉	201
⊟	660
◪	661
◀	521
⊐	D516
1	D501
2	592
3	593
▬	582
◣	584
/	690
\	691
6	692
⊤	693
Ξ	452
⊓	462
✳	642
T	883
▼	723
C	725
⫽	654
A	605
●	262

Materials for the Kingfisher
Hanging or Cushion

CANVAS:

gauge 10 holes per inch; measuring
20" x 20" which allows a 2" surround for
stretching. Actual size of work: 16" x 16".

PATERNA YARNS:

Black/ Charcoal 221, Dolphin D346,
D389, Steel Grey 201, Pine Green 660, 661,
Teal Blue 520, 521, Ocean Green D516,
Seafarer D501, Caribbean Blue 592, 593,
Sky Blue 582, 584, Loden Green 690, 691,
692, 693, Khaki Brwn 452, Beige Brown
462, Khaki Green 642, Ginger 883, Autumn
Yellow 723, 725, Olive Green 654, Forest
Green 605, White/Cream 262.

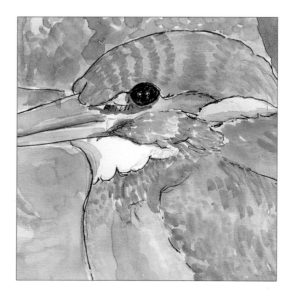

Once the work is stitched, it requires
stretching to its original shape and
dimensions, and then either making up
into a cushion with a deep frame, or a
small hanging (p. 157).

Photocopy chart x 183% for actual size of tapestry

Appendix

Materials

The basic materials required for the projects in this book are canvas, yarns and needles. This is one of the great attractions of needlepoint—the fact that you can create beautiful wall-hangings, pillows, cushions, chairs, seats and all manner of objects large and small with very little equipment.

CANVAS

This comes in many different varieties—single-thread, interlock and double-thread or Penelope canvas being the most widely available. Single-thread canvas comprises single threads woven under and over each other, which means that the fabric has plenty of "give." This makes it appropriate for cushions and pillows, but not for any surface that needs to stay taut, such as a chair seat. For these, interlock or double-thread canvas is best. Interlock is woven from single threads, but in such a way that they are fixed together at the points of intersection. This type of canvas particularly suits small pieces of needlepoint since it can be trimmed close to the stitched area without unravelling. In double-thread canvas, pairs of vertical threads intersect with pairs of horizontal threads. As well as being hardwearing, this double-mesh construction is useful when doing closely detailed work because you can use each thread singly in chosen areas, thereby giving yourself twice the number of holes per inch.

All the pieces in this book have been worked on double-thread canvas, of 10 holes per inch gauge, or 7.6 holes per inch for the larger designs. The more holes per inch, the finer the detail and the longer the work takes to stitch. It is a good idea to bear this in mind when buying canvas, so that when stitching you will progress at a rate that you can enjoy. Personally I find the larger-gauge canvases sufficient for an ample amount of detail.

Canvas comes in different shades and however well you stitch, there are always places where it shows slightly. This is why I always use a beige—usually called "antique"—canvas, whose color hardly shows when exposed between the stitches. Of course if you are working from a design in which the colors are extremely pale, it might be better to use white or cream.

YARN

Any kind of thread can be used in needlepoint, but the most common is wool. Tapestry wool, which forms a single strand, will cover most average gauges of canvas. Crewel wool is used singly on small gauges and with tapestry wool on larger gauges, but its commonest use is for petit point on finer-gauge canvas. The most versatile wool is Persian yarn. This is what I have used throughout the pieces in this book, from the Paterna range of yarns, which consist of three finer strands twisted together, each being approximately of equal weight to crewel yarn. On canvas with a gauge of 7.6 holes per inch I have worked with the complete 3 strands, and on 10 holes per inch I have used only two of the strands. The third I have saved to combine at a later date with the other extra strands. On pieces I have stitched for my personal use I have often used two or three different shades of wool twisted to form one strand to give more subtlety; but this would be too complicated on items that are to be charted.

NEEDLES

Tapestry needles have blunt ends in order to pass through the canvas without snagging. They come in many different sizes; the one mostly used on 10-gauge canvas is size 18. For 7.6-gauge canvas, size 16 is best.

Techniques

PREPARATION

The canvas should be cut approximately 2 inches larger all the way round than the size of the actual finished work. This allows a margin for stretching the piece back to its original proportions. The process of stitching distorts the canvas to some extent - much more so when tent stitch is used, because of its diagonal pull. But random long stitch also looks neater and more finished once it has been stretched out.

When cutting your canvas, always trim along one thread to save waste - it will unravel otherwise. It is useful to cover the raw edges with masking tape or sew bias binding onto them; this prevents the yarn from catching on them while you are stitching.

Make sure that throughout the process of stitching, the top of the canvas is identifiable in some way. This will safeguard against you resuming work after an interruption, only to start stitching it in the opposite direction.

Use lengths of yarn measuring up to 20 inches; anything longer will become weak and thin, leaving areas of canvas exposed between the stitches.

It is important to avoid using knots, since they create a lumpy texture and make it hard to stretch the work evenly. Make the first stitch so that with your other hand you are holding a 5-inch length of yarn firmly on the underside of the canvas. Keep holding this tail of thread while you

pull the first stitch firm; then continue so that the next few stitches can be worked over the loose yarn, making it invisible. The same effect can be achieved when finishing off, by darning the remains of the thread under the stitching and cutting off any remainder.

On a canvas designed with several areas in the same colour, often you can run the thread under the stitching from one patch to another. But it is advisable to cut the yarn and start again, when two such areas are any distance apart.

Some people like to stitch on a frame so that the work distorts less, but I prefer not to because it is quicker, and easier to put the work up on a wall and see how it is going. If you do want to use one you can make it readily enough with four stretchers of the kind used in mounting canvas for painting. All you need to do is to buy four stretchers of the required length and width and mount the canvas on it, using tacks. Work outwards from the centre, pulling the canvas taut as you do so (p. 95).

USING CHARTS

Those used in this book are box charts, where each square represents one stitch. The squares contain symbols to indicate the colour of the yarns used. The larger squares on the box charts represent one canvas intersection – i.e., a vertical thread and a horizontal thread intersecting – not a hole in the canvas. As noted at the front of this book, these box charts are much easier to use if photocopied up to the actual size of the needlepoint to be stitched.

STITCHING

The two basic stitches used for the needlepoints in this book are Tent Stitch and Random Long Stitch. Tent Stitch is worked diagonally over only one intersection of the canvas. The needle always covers at least two threads on the wrong side of the work, which makes it a very durable stitch. Random Long Stitch is a straight stitch which lies parallel to the canvas threads. It is ideal for filling large areas of canvas quickly, as it is worked in varying lengths along each row. It is worked row by row, alternating from left to right then from right to left, with the rows interlocking.

STRETCHING AND SIZING

Stretching actually means bringing your finished work back to its original proportions. If it is a square cushion worked in tent stitch, it will look more like a parallelogram by the time it is finished. But by stretching you can return it to its square or rectangular shape.

First you will need a piece of board able to take one-and-a-half-inch or two-inch rustproof nails. It will have to be at least three inches larger all the way round than the actual worked area.

Place some plain undyed fabric on the board, then lay the finished work face down on this. Dampen the wrong side of the work with a mister or a moistened sponge and pull roughly into shape. As a guide, you can make a template from paper or card, or you can keep measuring with a ruler, using a set square to make sure that the corners form right angles. I usually hammer the first nail into the centre of one side, working out along that edge and then doing the other three sides. Once I am satisfied with the measurements, and the angles of the corners, I add nails until the edges are suitably straight and the nails are less than an inch apart.

Size the back evenly with wallpaper paste. This gives the work body and helps it to retain its shape better. Leave in a warm place for at least forty-eight hours, until absolutely dry. The nails can then be pulled out with the claw of a hammer, and the work made up into its final form.

CUSHIONS AND PILLOWS

Cut the backing fabric with a half-inch seam allowance in addition to the area of the needlepoint. To allow for any zip, cut the backing as two equal pieces with a further seam allowance for the zip measuring five-eighths of an inch on each half. Stitch the top and bottom one-and-three-quarter inches of the seam for the zip. Baste the remainder. Following the instructions supplied with the zip, insert the zip into the basted part of the seam.

With right sides together, pin the backing to the needlepoint. Machine stitch, keeping close to the needlepoint, along three edges, or four if you have included a zip. Having turned the cushion cover right side out, you can now insert the cushion pad. Zip up the cover or oversew the fourth edge by hand.

HANGINGS

To mitre the corners of a finished hanging, all excess canvas must be trimmed to within about one-and-a-quarter inches of the stitching. With the wrong side facing you, fold the corner towards the centre of the canvas, and press. Fold the other two edges and neatly oversew the edges with herringbone stitch on the back of the work.

The hanging can then either be framed in fabric or just backed, leaving one inch unstitched at the top corners so that a rod can be inserted which can then be suspended from nails or hooks.

PLACEMATS

In addition to protecting the surface of the fabric against spillages, it is a good idea to add a backing, in a heat-absorbent material such as felt or cork. Cut the backing to the size and shape of the canvas. With a steam iron, press the canvas across the corners of the needlepoint. Fold both sides of each corner and bring the edges to-gether to make a neat diagonal seam on the wrong side of the canvas. Press again and sew this down using herringbone stitch.

Sew the felt down, hemming it under on the back of the needlepoint with small stitches, so that you pick up threads of canvas rather than needlepoint stitches.

S u p p l i e r s

YARNS

United States:

Johnson's Creative Arts Inc., 35 Scales Lane, Townsend,

Massachusetts 01469, tel. (508) 597-8794.

Canada:

Kelsea Sales, 585 Middlefield Road, Unit 30, Scarborough, Ontario, M1V 4Y5,

tel. (416) 298-0443

CANVAS

United States:

Dimensions, 641 MacKnight Street, Reading, Pennsylvania, 19601-2499,

tel. (610) 372-8491.

Canada:

Coats Patons, 1001 Roselawn Avenue, Toronto, Ontario, M6B 1B8,

tel. (416) 782-4481.

BUTTERFLY FIRESCREEN FRAME

Stitchery, 6 High Street, Thames Ditton, Surrey KT7 0RY, tel. 081 398 5550.

HOLLYHOCK SCREEN FRAME

David Jackson-Hulme, Handmade Country Furniture, Field House Farm,

Onecote, Leek, Staffs., ST13 7SD, tel. 01538 304542. Mail order from U.K.

only.

KITS

United States:

The following designs are available as kits in the United States from Ehrman,

5 Northern Boulevard, Amherst, Massachusetts, 03031, tel. (800) 433-7899,

and in Canada from Pointers, 1017 Mount Pleasant Road, Toronto, Ontario,

M4P 2M1, tel. (416) 322-9461: Dark Auricula cushion, Irises and Delphiniums

hanging, English Landscape Tuscan Landscape, Heraldic cushion, Butterfly

firescreen

B o o k   L i s t

Auriculas—Their Care and Cultivation, Brenda Hyatt, Cassell, 1989.

Birds, Beasts, Blossoms and Bugs, Harold P. Stern, Abrams, 1976.

British Butterflies and their Transformations, H. N. Humphreys and J. O. Westwood, 1851.

Fruits of the Earth, Hugh Ehrman, Century, 1991.

Glorious Inspiration, Kaffe Fassett, Century, 1991.

Glorious Needlepoint, Kaffe Fassett, Century Hutchinson, 1987.

The Glory of the English Garden, Mary Keen, with photographs by Clay Perry, Barrie & Jenkins, 1991.

Great Flower Books 1700–1900, Sacheverell Sitwell, H. F. & G. Witherby Ltd, 1990.

The Illustrated History of Textiles, ed. Madeleine Ginsbury, Studio Editions, 1991.

Kaffe Fassett at the V & A, Century, 1988.

Ocean Life: Beneath the Crystal Seas, Vic Cox, The Image Bank, 1989.

Tile Art, Noel Riley, Apple Press/Quintet, 1987.

Traditional English Gardens, Lennox-Boyd, Perry, Thomas, National Trust in association with Weidenfeld and Nicolson, 1987.

The Victoria and Albert Museum's Textile Collection—Embroidery in Britain from 1200 to 1750, Victoria & Albert Museum, 1993.

Conversion Table

The tapestries in this book have all been stitched with Paterna yarns. For suppliers in the U.K., U.S.A., Canada and Australia, write to Paterna, M.P. Stonehouse Ltd., P.O. Box 13, Albion Mills, Wakefield, West Yorkshire WF2 9SG.

The conversion table below suggests DMC and Anchor yarns in shades comparable to the Paterna yarn numbers. However, as the shades and tones of the yarns produced by the three companies differ quite widely, the appearance of the finished tapestries will be affected if alternative yarns are used.

Paterna	DMC	Anchor	Paterna	DMC	Anchor	Paterna	DMC	Anchor	Paterna	DMC	Anchor
201	7626	9794	500	7297	8632	651	7425	9310	833	7214	8234
210	7713	8720	501	7591	8630	652	7363	9308	842	7606	8214
211	7284	8718	504	7593	8628	653	7361	9306	843	7850	8212
213	7715	8712	505	7313	8624	654	7371	9302	844	7851	8306
220	7309	9800	510	7288	8840	660	7389	9028	845	7852	8302
221	7624	9768	515	7301	8816	661	7387	8974	851	7920	8238
256	7300	9784	520	7327	8924	662	7541	9020	852	7125	8234
260	White	8000	521	7326	8922	664	7542	9014	855	7917	8232
261/2/3	Ecru	8002/4/6	522	7598	8918	670	7583	9198	862	7356	8262
301	7708	8526	530	7429	8906	671	7584	9274	863	7124	8258
311	7242	8528	551	7317	8674	690	7379	9208	870	7169	8352
313	7241	8544	552	7316	8672	691	7367	9206	874	7164	8344
320	7259	8514	553	7313	8776	692	7388	9198	883	7919	9556
321	7257	8512	555	7301	8772	693	7548	9196	885	7192	9532
326	7132	9612	560	7555	8644	694	7549	9194	900	7219	8426
332	7243	8590	571	7318	8636	700	7767	8024	902	7138	8424
334	7241	8584	580	7311	8824	710	7784	8100	903	7602	8422
340	7796	8612	581	7650	8822	711	7785	8098	904	7603	8416
341	7797	8610	582	7995	8808	712	7726	8018	906	7133	8416
342	7798	8608	583	7813	8806	713	7727	8016	910	7212	8426
343	7799	8604	584	7996	8804	720	7401	8064	913	7204	8366
344	7800	8602	585	7828	8802	722	7445	9526	922	7217	8350
351	7155	8490	592	7807	8938	723	7444	8140	940	7137	8442
353	7153	8488	593	7598	8936	725	7506	8136	950	7544	8218
400	7449	9496	601	7890	9080	727	7078	8112	970	7107	8202
410	7467	9644	604	7402	9074	731	7833	8062	D115	7238	9684
413	7918	9554	605	7400	9072	732	7474	8022	D281	7194	8396
421	7489	9618	610	7385	9008	733	7494	8042	D346	7705	9776
432	7497	9682	611	7320	9006	743	7503	8018	D389	7285	9774
433	7780	9392	612	7384	9004	745	7579	8052	D411	7700	9450
441	7513	9408	613	7382	9002	751	7781	8044	D419	7176	9448
451	7490	9314	640	7417	9223	752	7783	8042	D501	7956	8968
452	7514	9312	641	7425	9220	754	7745	8038	D511	7355	9312
461	7416	9372	642	7355	9216	755	7905	8036	D516	7428	8992
462	7413	9366	643	7423	9214	762	7431	8092	D521	7676	9216
494	7171	9612	644	7493	9304	764	7905	8012			